Ordinary People

Extraordinary Stories

Published by Crossbridge Books
Worcester WR6 6PL
www.crossbridgeeducational.com

©Crossbridge Books 2023

All rights reserved. No part of this publication
may be reproduced, stored in a retrieval system,
or transmitted in any form or by any means –
electronic, mechanical, photocopying, recording
or otherwise – without prior permission of the
Copyright owner.

ISBN 978 1 913946 94 4

British Library Cataloguing in Publication Data
A catalogue record for this book is available from the British Library

Scripture taken from the New King James Version®. Copyright © 1982
by Thomas Nelson. Used by permission. All rights reserved.

 CROSSBRIDGE BOOKS

Ordinary People

Extraordinary Stories

Leslene Peat-Brown

'The Lord your God, who goes before you, He will fight for you, according to all He did for you in Egypt before your eyes, and in the wilderness where you saw how the Lord your God carried you, as a man carries his son, in all the way that you went until you came to this place. Yet for all that, you did not believe the Lord your God, who went in the way before you.' (Deuteronomy 1:30-33)

About the Author

Leslene Peat-Brown is the senior elder in her local church where she has been prayer leader for several years. She holds an Honours degree in Psychology, and an MA in Education.

Contents: **Page:**

Foreword	1
Introduction	2
God Heals:	5
O'Neil's Story - One Night to Live	6
Samantha's Story - Keep on Running	13
Annette's Story - God and God Alone	18
Stan's Story - Nothing is Impossible with God	24
Amanda's Story - Do you Believe that God can Heal You?	27
Esther's Story - A Call for Help.	30
God Provides:	33
Flo's Story - I Believe in Miracles	34
Hannah-Mae's Story – Elderberries	36
Jane's Story - The Hidden Bank Account	38
Ann's Story - Miracles and More Miracles	40
Helen's Story - God's Plan	44
God Cares:	49
Ron's Story - Ride with an Angel	50
Elizabeth's Story - The Carpet Cleaner	53
Elizabeth's Story - Trip to South Wales	55
Rick's Story - A Very Present Help	57
Ruth's Story - When you Least Expect	59

Foreword

As I listen to the testimonies of fellow believers, I have come to appreciate the tremendous power of prayer, and I can also attest to being inspired by them; but more importantly, prayer has become an integral part of my life. It is through prayer and study of God's word that I am being drawn closer to Him, as He recreates me into His likeness daily.

I am constantly being blessed by the testimonies of ordinary people, some of whom have encountered many challenges in their lives. I am pleased to have the opportunity, with their permission, to share some of their testimonies. It is my desire that you will be blessed through reading their stories, and that your faith in God will be strengthened as mine has been over the years.

These stories are in themselves miracles. I firmly believe that I have been led by the Holy Spirit to share with others that even though we are living in a world of chaos and confusion that God still answers prayers; He still works miracles, miracles that did not end with the disciples in the New Testament - they continue to this day.

I pray that the stories in this book will not only inspire you, but also ignite in you a passion for God as you develop your faith, and a growing relationship with Him.

Introduction

Reading about the life of Christ and the early disciples, I realise how privileged we are as Christians to be chosen to be part of God's plan to evangelise the world. It is through the lives that we live in Christ that we can testify to others of His might and power to transform lives. This is the very essence of what He requires of us. 'And this gospel of the kingdom will be preached in the world as a **witness [testimony]** to all nations, and then the end will come.' (Matthew 24:14). This commission includes both corporate and personal testimonies in discipling others.

Ordinary People, Extraordinary Stories is a compilation of testimonies from family, friends, and fellow believers.

When I interviewed those who willingly and excitedly told me their stories, I became more convinced that, even in the twenty first century, God continues to work miracles in the lives of men and women. Despite challenges to their faith, they persisted in prayer, believing that God would bring about change. In some instances, their situation appeared impossible. However, these testimonies are evidence that it is only God who can make the impossible possible.

During my time as prayer leader in my church, I listened to various testimonies of believers who, because of their love for God and faith in Him, were able to overcome challenges in their lives and surmount difficulties. Despite challenges to their faith, they believed that God would answer their prayers, and He did in ways that were truly amazing.

The more I heard their testimonies the more convinced I became that others needed to hear them too, hence the compilation of testimonies that you are now reading. Listening to these testimonies I was often overwhelmed by the persistence in prayer that each person displayed, even in seemingly impossible situations. Some waited years before receiving answers from God, but their faith would not allow them to cease praying. It was evident to me that they had a relationship with God that helped to sustain their faith.

These testimonies have not only inspired me to compile this book, but they have also impacted my life, whereby my faith in God has been strengthened. I have also learnt to be more persistent in prayer, and I am beginning to understand more clearly what Jesus means when He says, "Ask, and it will be given to you; seek, and you will find; knock, and it will be opened to you. For everyone who asks receives; and he who seeks finds, and to him who knocks it will be opened." (Matthew 7:7-8)

I have also learnt the importance of interceding in prayer for others. I am guided by the instruction Paul gave Timothy: "I exhort first of all that supplications, prayers, intercessions, and giving of thanks be made for all men," (1Timothy 2:1).

It is my desire that these testimonies will impact your life as they have mine. I pray that you will have a greater appreciation for God and His Word, and to begin to understand how special you are to Him. I am amazed that God, who is all mighty, all powerful, and all knowing, has chosen us to help to change lives through the power of prayer and our personal testimonies.

When I listened to these testimonies of God's miraculous intervention in the lives of those who have contributed their stories, I now have a greater appreciation of the truth that God requires faith in Him and consistency and commitment in prayer. When we exercise faith in Him, it always brings good results. In Hebrews 11:6, we are reminded that: 'he who comes to God must believe that He is, and that He is a rewarder of those who diligently seek Him.'

I can identify with some of these testimonies; I have learnt that you might find yourself in a seemingly impossible situation, however, God still works miracles. He brings hope all the time to situations that appear hopeless and impossible.

As you read these testimonies may you be encouraged and strengthened as you put your trust in the only One who works with impossibilities.

God Heals

O'Neil's Story – One Night to Live

'The effective, fervent prayer of a righteous man avails much.'

(James 5:16)

As a young boy growing up with my siblings on one of the beautiful Caribbean islands, life was full of fun and laughter. I was happy and excited about the future. However, little did I know that my life and that of my family was about to change drastically.

From the age of sixteen I began experiencing headaches which I thought were just migraines, therefore I did not pay much attention to them. However, as the months went by, they became increasingly worse, and by the time I was eighteen years old my health began to deteriorate, and my appetite was poor, which resulted in substantial weight loss.

My mother and I became more and more concerned about my worsening health as the headaches intensified. I knew something was wrong and became very anxious and scared.

My mother sought help from many doctors, but none was able to diagnose my condition, let alone administer treatment. After having had several blood tests, X rays and scans, I was eventually referred to a specialist - the very best on the island, however, at a very high financial cost. We do not have a National Health Service on the island, which means that everyone pays for health care.

I can recall the morning my mother and I boarded the taxi to visit the specialist. I was very apprehensive, not knowing what the outcome would be. I prayed silently that the doctor would be able to make a diagnosis. Although we were not members of a church, my mother ensured my siblings and I learnt how to pray and attend church every Sunday. Sometimes we would even attend the local Seventh-day Adventist church on a Saturday. Strangely enough, mother sent us to church, however, she seldom attended herself.

As we continued our journey, I felt somewhat reassured, considering that the specialist was the best on the island, and thought surely, he would be able to find out what was wrong with me. Feeling optimistic, I settled down to enjoy the journey.

We arrived at the surgery on time but had to wait before we could be seen. As we sat waiting, I could feel my heart pounding hard against my chest as I thought, 'What if this doctor, like all the others, cannot find anything wrong with me, and if he did, would it be good news or bad news?' These were the thoughts that occupied my mind.

We hadn't waited for long, but it seemed like an eternity. Suddenly, I could hear the nurse calling my name and we were finally ushered in to see the doctor. He read my notes, and asked several questions as he took my history. After having read the results of the various tests I had had, he examined me. My mother and I sat in quiet anticipation as he wrote in my notes. Finally, he looked up at us and spoke rather hesitantly, as if trying to find the right words to say.

I remember the look of horror on my mother's face when he broke the news that I had a malignant condition that was very advanced, and that I had only a matter of days to live.

I sat there 'frozen' with fear and wondered, 'Did I hear him mention the word death?' My mind was now in a whirl, and I wondered if it was playing tricks on me, or was this real? 'Was my life ebbing away from me as I sat in the surgery?'

We left the surgery, and as we made our way home, neither of us spoke, however, mother had a worried look on her face. As we travelled in the taxi, I would sometimes take sideway glances at her, but we avoided looking at each other.

A few days after we had seen the specialist, my mother announced that we would be seeing yet another doctor for a second opinion. Little did I know that this second medical consultation would result in a chain of events that would change my life forever.

As we went to see the doctor, I felt somewhat hopeful and prayed that the diagnosis would be different, but this was not the case as my worst fears were confirmed. The doctor examined me and, (it would appear, he had no training in psychology) as he looked my mother in the eye said, "He'll be lucky if he makes it through the night". We left the surgery feeling totally dejected, scared, hopeless and helpless. I couldn't help thinking, 'I have just started living.' My whole life was ahead of me; I was petrified at the doctor's words. I felt as if all the blood had suddenly drained from my body; I was crippled with fear as I sensed that the doctor was literally sending me home to die at the age of eighteen. It was unfair that my life should end this way. I was a good lad who never gave mother any trouble, everyone in my community knew me as a helpful and respectful young man.

The journey home was an unusually quiet one. Mother was distraught, yet she said nothing. As for me, I was too frightened to speak. Once again, mother and I avoided looking at each other. However, she did something that was unusual when we stopped at a nearby shop and bought me a treat, a bottle of fizzy drink! I would normally share a bottle of drink with my siblings, but now I had the entire bottle for myself, I really felt special.

Shortly after we arrived home, news soon spread about my poor health. Family members and neighbours started gathering at our house for a vigil. Everyone stayed overnight. No one slept; it was as if they were waiting for me to die.

My mother had no formal education but was incredibly hardworking and ran her own business. She was very astute, was good at planning ahead, forthright, and expressed herself frankly. She was a wise woman and gave us good counsel. However, she rarely showed her emotions, and if challenged by situations or circumstances, would quickly rise above them, but this time I could see the pain of my condition etched on her face. She appeared so fragile.

As people gathered in our house, I was afraid of going to sleep and remembered my sister praying and crying as she sat on my bed. At one point she cried so loudly that mother came rushing in, she too began to cry. This was the first time I had ever seen her cry; this strong and resilient woman was now broken.

As more people gathered, my sister Susan called everyone to prayer. They began to sing and pray and read promises from the Bible. As they did, the atmosphere in my bedroom changed. I felt less fearful, experienced an indescribable peace, and finally fell asleep.

I woke up the next morning and one can only imagine my joy of being alive. I made it through the night; I had defied the doctors! There were so many people that morning greeting me; they too were happy that I was alive. This was truly the best morning of all mornings that I had ever spent on planet earth! It was such joy to wake up to so many people greeting me and wishing me good morning.

Slowly, family members and neighbours left, and as they did my family and I reflected on what had taken place that night. I felt so much better and even had breakfast! I had not eaten for several days.

As we sat recounting the events of the night, there was a knock on the door. It was a group of seven ladies from the local Seventh-day Adventist church. Apparently, it was customary for them to meet on Wednesdays to fast and pray from sunrise to sunset. However, during the prayer session one member of the group felt impressed to go into the community to pray for those who were sick.

Shortly after arriving at our door, they told us that they had come to pray for me. I was asked to pray quietly for myself and confess my sins, which I did. I remained on my knees as the ladies encircled me and began to pray. I had never ever heard such prayers like the prayers of those seven ladies, as they interceded on my behalf. They prayed with such fervour, faith, and strong belief that God would hear their prayers. I can recall them quoting the words of James, "The prayer of a righteous person is powerful and effective".

As they prayed, I felt a surge of what I can only describe as blood running through every vessel and fibre of my body, the kind of feeling I experienced when I was baptised. At the end of the prayer session, I stood up and with tears flowing down my cheeks, I heard myself saying, "I am healed, I am healed! Thank God, thank God."

Whatever I was suffering from was no longer there. Those women of faith said confidently, "Yes, we know you have been healed." Shortly after that, they left.

As a result of my miraculous healing, I gave my life to Christ and joined the prayer group where I witnessed many more miracles in answer to our prayers.

What the doctors, and the only specialist on the island, could not do for me, God did! What a great and powerful God we serve. Nothing is impossible for Him.

My Commitment:

On the day of my healing, I made a commitment with God that wherever I went, and whoever I met, I would tell them what God did for me that day. When the death sentence, "Only one night to live" was passed, My God intervened and saved my life by healing me of a terminal illness. I will glorify His name and speak of His mighty healing power as long as I live. I cannot keep silent for He has done a great and marvellous thing in my life which makes me glad.

May God bless you as you read my story. (O'Neil)

Samantha's Story - Keep on Running

The story of Samantha Dewar as told by her father.

'In my distress I cried to the Lord, and He heard me.'

(Psalm 120:1)

I will never forget July 15th, 2011. My daughter Samantha had successfully repeated her seven times multiplication table, and as a treat she was allowed to go shopping with her aunt in the second largest city on the island where we lived.

They had an exciting trip to the city that day and it was now time to return home. They boarded a mini-bus and were soon on their way. The journey started well, until it began to rain heavily, and before you knew it a thunderstorm had developed. At approximately 2:30 pm, a tree which had been struck by lightning fell on the top of the minibus. So great was the impact that a passenger sitting next to Samantha was instantly killed. Fortunately for Samantha, her aunt and the other passengers who were not injured were able to walk from the wreckage to seek assistance.

They were all taken to the local hospital and examined for any injuries. However, upon arriving at the hospital, Samantha began complaining of numbness and lack of feeling from her diaphragm to her feet. She was examined by the doctor immediately, who ordered an Xray which revealed that she had sustained damage to her spinal cord. Samantha needed surgery. Unfortunately, there wasn't a resident neurologist at the hospital, so she had to be airlifted to the University Teaching Hospital on the other side of the island for surgery.

The surgery went well, but when Samantha recovered, she was still unable to experience any feeling in her legs. I was greatly concerned for my daughter and feared she would never walk again. Recovery seemed slow; it was painful to see her just lying on the bed unable to move her legs. She was at her lowest, physically, and emotionally. I wished that I could have traded places with her.

Two weeks had passed since her surgery, yet still there was no improvement. The medical staff, not seeing any improvement, gave up hope of her ever being able to walk again. You can imagine how devastated we were with this prognosis. I was beside myself with worry and anxiety, however, I was not losing hope. Samantha was later referred to the Rehabilitation Centre for physiotherapy. During this time, I kept on praying and reading God's promises in the Bible.

It was at this point that I asked for a consultation with the neurologist. In our discussion, he said that so far Samantha had not shown any signs of improvement despite having had surgery; he concluded that she would never walk again. I became overwhelmed by what he said, despair and dread and hopelessness had overcome me. I could not bear the thought of my child in a wheelchair for the rest of her life. It was then that I prayed a silent prayer to God for help.

As I left his surgery, I thanked the doctor for being honest and candid, however, I told him that I could not accept the prognosis that my daughter would never walk again. Although it was quite evident to me that she would never walk again, I heard myself telling him, "I believe that my daughter will walk again. I am confident that one day she will walk into your practice."

Samantha, who was now paralysed from the waist down, was assessed for rehabilitation on the 2nd of August 2011, and admitted to the centre the following day for therapy. However, there was more sad news to come. The centre manager informed me that they could not commence therapy until she experienced movements in her legs; the best they could do for her was to teach her how to use a wheelchair to help with her mobility. I was disappointed but not discouraged as I had left the matter in God's hands. The more I prayed the more I felt certain that Samantha would walk again. I felt in my heart, soul, and every fibre in my body, that God was about to birth a miracle and that my little girl would walk again.

Every day, morning, and every evening I would sit by my daughter's bedside praying, massaging, and anointing her legs, while others all over the world were also praying and interceding with God for her healing. The strength gained through this period of worry and anxiety helped to strengthen my faith in God, and I knew He would answer our prayers.

On one occasion when I was praying, Samantha asked, "Daddy will I ever walk again?" Without hesitation, I replied, "Yes Samantha, you will walk again. Do you believe you will walk again Samantha?" "Yes daddy," she replied, "I will walk again." We prayed together and claimed God's promises, believing in faith that He would heal her.

After two months of praying and massaging Samantha's legs, she began to experience feeling in her thighs and feet, and by October she was moving her toes, two on the right and three on the left foot. I was overcome with joy and ran to tell the Physiotherapist what I had observed. However, I was told that they were "just spasms." I insisted that she should come with me to see Samantha. I asked Samantha to move her toes and she did. The Physiotherapist was amazed and apologised for doubting me. She began intense physiotherapy with Samantha who began to improve daily. As the therapy progressed, Samantha was now beginning to stand without support.

A few weeks later we attended an appointment with the neurosurgeon who had performed the operation. On arrival at the clinic, I asked her to stand from her wheelchair, which she did. The surgeon could not believe what he was seeing, considering this was the girl he said would never walk again! He and his team were amazed. In fact, for a moment, he was lost for words, before stating that in 1 out of 1,000 cases recovery can happen as was evident in Samantha's case. I replied, "This might be so, but as far as I am concerned this is an answer to prayer. It is the hand of God that works miracles."

After receiving six months of intense therapy, Samantha returned to school, not just walking but running. The teachers were amazed. It seemed no one could stop her from running, it was as if she had a completely new set of legs! She caught up well with her lessons and was successful in her grade four literacy exams.

I cannot stop praising and thanking God for the miracle he performed on my daughter. May all thanks be given to the One and Only true God, the Great Healer. I would like to express my gratitude to all those who prayed for her recovery.

Samantha is now studying at university to become a physiotherapist.

Annette's Story – God and God Alone.

'When you pass through the waters, I will be with you; and through the rivers, they shall not overflow you. When you walk through the fire, you shall not be burned, nor shall the flame scorch you.'

(Isaiah 43:2)

It was the third of November 1998. For reasons unknown to me I felt very tired and exhausted most of the time, and this became increasingly worse when I was unable to drive myself home one day. A friend kindly drove me home.

On arriving home, I slumped onto the couch and remembered nothing thereafter until I woke up in hospital. I was told that I had had a Grand Mal epileptic fit. I was kept in hospital for a few days for observations and was later discharged home. However, the convulsions continued, but they were Petit mal seizures, occurring approximately four times per week.

Although I was still experiencing tiredness and exhaustion, by February 1999 I was able to travel abroad to my step grandmother's funeral. Whilst there, I frequently felt dizzy but thought nothing of it, and concluded that it might have been the heat of the sun that was giving rise to the dizzy spells. However, one day my aunt, who had been observing me, commented on my unsteady gait. I explained to her that I had been feeling dizzy and unwell, to which she replied, "Oh, be positive." I thought this was a very odd response.

Two weeks later, after arriving home, I woke up from sleep feeling dizzier than I had ever felt before. It appeared that everything in my bedroom was moving - the ceiling, the walls, and the floor were like a whirlpool. I attempted to go to the bathroom, but as I tried to stand, I found I was unable to, lost my balance and fell to the floor. Eventually, with help, I managed to get up. Not understanding what was happening to me I prayed to God for strength. Not only did He strengthen me, but He also gave me the ability to 'furniture walk,' (in other words, holding on to furniture for support).

My condition began to worsen; I became unable to walk and I could not chew my food without biting my lips and cheeks. I dreaded every mealtime as I was experiencing difficulties in swallowing. I had to pray when it was time to eat.

During this time, my sight became impaired. I began seeing double; people and objects were constantly moving as the dizzy spells continued. My speech became slurred, becoming increasingly worse each day, and my memory was impaired. The doctors commenced various investigations but had not yet made a diagnosis.

It was now the year 2000, and despite my medical condition I had planned to attend a conference in Toronto. However, I was advised by the doctors not to travel.

One day, after spending much time in prayer, God spoke to me and told me to fast from food and liquids for three days. After this fast I was weak, and after having had some soup, I was again instructed to fast for another three days, this time, consuming fruits, and water only. At the end of this second fast I was once more instructed to continue fasting for a further three days, having water, fruits, and vegetables.

On the eighth day, I cried out to the Lord, saying, "I can't go on anymore." I was weak and exhausted by now. It appeared that I was getting worse, and not better as anticipated. I was really at my lowest.

It was during that moment of despair that the telephone rang; it was my mother calling from Toronto. She had attended a workshop at the conference where a doctor had been speaking about a condition similar to mine. Based on his research findings and what he had said in his presentation, my mother had called to tell me to change my diet. I told her I had already done so after having spent nine days fasting, under the direction of the Holy Spirit. I told her that I was already consuming large portions of fruits and green leafy vegetables only. Although swallowing was still difficult, I was persisting.

After numerous investigations, the doctors finally diagnosed cerebellar ataxia. This is a disorder of the brain that occurs when the cerebellum becomes inflamed or damaged. The cerebellum is the area of the brain responsible for controlling gait and muscle coordination. The term ataxia refers to a lack of fine control of voluntary movements.

My consultant at the Royal National Hospital where I was a patient, had by now referred me to a neurologist in Sheffield who had been conducting research into cerebellar ataxia. He wanted me to participate in his study.

However, when the neurologist saw me, he exclaimed, "What has happened?" My response was, "You are the doctor, you should be telling me." He then continued by saying, "But the information I have on your file is inconsistent with the woman I am looking at. According to your condition, you should have been totally bedridden by now." At that point I informed him that I was a praying Christian and that might be the reason for the difference he was seeing in me. (He obviously expected me to be in a far worse state, knowing the extent of the condition.) I also told him about my fasting and change of diet which might have also contributed to the change he saw in my illness. When I had finished speaking, he said, "Talk about Divine intervention! There's nothing else I can do for you," he said. "I'll send you back to London. As you are aware, your condition is a progressive degenerative illness." He asked about my diet and suggested I should seek further advice from the dietitian.

Shortly after my return from Sheffield, the dietitian contacted me, and we discussed my diet. It was then that I was informed that the recent biopsies, lumbar puncture, and other investigations that I had, revealed protein in my tissues and cerebrospinal fluid. I can recall saying to her that protein was good for the body, so why was that a concern. "Yes, but not when it is present in the tissues and cerebrospinal fluid," she replied.

"As well as the diagnosis of cerebellar ataxia, you also have an intolerance to gluten, wheat, barley, and oats, which could also be having a damaging effect on your cerebellum," she explained.

After our conversation ended, I collapsed on the floor, crying, not feeling sorry for myself, but praying and giving thanks to God for His leading, His care, and protection; for directing me every step of the journey through my illness. He even changed my taste buds to the extent that foods that I had previously disliked, were now more palatable. I thank Him daily for providing the best diet for me.

Although I am still unable to walk and need a wheelchair to get around, I often tell myself and others that, "I'd rather go to heaven in a wheelchair than to walk into hell!" My speech is much improved, so is my swallowing. As my illness progressed, it affected my memory, in fact it was non-existent; I couldn't even remember my children's names! However, my God, who has been faithful to me and continues to be, instructed me to memorise scripture if I wanted to get my memory back. Initially, it took me one year to learn Genesis 1:1 'In the beginning God created the heavens and the earth!' Now I can quote books, chapters, and verses of the Bible! Thank God for giving me back my memory.

As I reflect on my life so far, I want to thank God for the way He has led me through this very difficult period in my life. It is God, and God alone, who has healed me thus far. If He chooses to bring about complete healing, then may His will be done. If he chooses not to, I will by His grace, 'glory in my infirmities.' Whatever happens, I will continue to trust Him because He has given me this beautiful promise,

> 'When you pass through the waters, I will be with you; and through the rivers, they shall not overflow you. When you walk through the fire, you shall not be burned, nor shall the flame scorch you.' (Isaiah 43:2).

He has certainly kept His promise.

It is now the year 2023 and I am still alive. Thank God.

Stan's Story - Nothing is Impossible with God

'This poor man cried out, and the Lord heard him and saved him out of all his troubles.'

(Psalm 34:6)

Throughout my life I have been blessed with good health. You can therefore imagine my horror when in 2018 I began to experience health challenges which were quite severe and at the same time very frightening.

I made several visits to my General Practitioner who eventually referred me to a specialist at the local Teaching Hospital. After having undergone several investigations, which were all negative, the doctors were still unable to make a diagnosis and so I was discharged from their care.

However, the symptoms persisted, and as I tried to make sense of what was happening to me, I concluded that I was under attack from the evil one. Although I had been seeking the Lord in prayer for healing, it was then that I decided to seek Him more earnestly, asking for His intervention, through a 'Planned Prayer Programme.'

I discontinued the use of all medication that the doctor had prescribed, having made the decision to rely solely on God, and embarked upon the prayer programme. Armed with His promise, I began the programme.

> "Be strong and of good courage; do not be afraid, nor be dismayed, for the Lord God is with you wherever you go." (Joshua 1: 9)

The programme consisted of twenty-one days of fasting from 6am-6pm, without food during this period. For the last three days of the fast, I consumed no food or water. During this time, I spent time reading and meditating on the Scriptures and claimed God's promises. I remember claiming many promises, however the promise found in Deuteronomy 31:6 spoke to me in a powerful way,

> "He will not leave you nor forsake you."

I also meditated on Ephesians 6: 10-20, which speaks about the Christian life in which we battle against evil forces, however, we are encouraged that God will fight for us so we should not be discouraged because we will be victorious.

> 'For we do not wrestle against flesh and blood, but against principalities, against powers, against the rulers of the darkness of this age, against spiritual hosts of wickedness in the heavenly places. Therefore take up the whole armour of God, that you may be able to withstand in the

evil day, and having done all, to stand.' (Ephesians 6:12-13)

During each waking moment I spent time praying, praising, and giving thanks to God because I knew he would heal me. Psalms 90 and 91 also brought me much comfort and hope.

Throughout these intense prayer and fasting sessions, I felt God's presence with me, and knew that He would bring about healing in my life, not just physically but also spiritually too. During the programme, I kept praying at every available moment, even when I was driving! When the programme ended, I can testify that I was a new man. All my symptoms had disappeared, God had heard and answered my prayers; I was healed! Even now, as I recall this experience, I am still giving God thanks for what He did for me. Truly, nothing is too hard for God. He is faithful and will always keep His promises.

Since experiencing God's healing, I have recommended this programme to help and support others in need of healing.

Prayer remains an underutilised 'weapon' by Christians. I can assure anyone reading my testimony that God still answers prayer in a powerful way so long as we exercise faith, believing that nothing is impossible with Him. I continue to worship and adore Him for what He has done, and is still doing, in my life.

Amanda's Story - Do you Believe that God can Heal You?

"And the prayer of faith will save the sick, and the Lord will raise him up".

(James 5:15).

Mr Johnstone had been ill for several years and had little hope of getting better. As his illness progressed, he developed sores on his head, was unable to walk, and had only limited communication skills, to the extent of being incoherent at times. He was unable to care for himself; his main carers being his wife and daughter.

As a result of his disabilities, his home had to be adapted to suit his needs. His lounge was converted into a bedroom where he spent all his time. His only contact with the outside world was the scenery through his bedroom window.

Despite medical treatment for his physical condition, Mr Johnstone's family became more and more concerned about his mental health, which was slowly deteriorating; they considered whether they should request a psychological assessment. However, being practising Christians, they decided to request prayer from their minister and bishop on his behalf instead. Both the minister and the bishop visited Mr Johnstone on several occasions and prayed with him, but his condition remained unchanged. The medication from his doctor was now becoming ineffective and at times made his condition worse.

It was during this time that a friend, who regularly visited, asked Mr Johnstone if he minded having the minister from his church pray for him. Apparently, the minister was from a Sabbath-keeping church, however, Mr Johnstone readily accepted, and even revealed that he believed in the seventh-day Sabbath as being the correct day of worship.

Arrangements were made for the pastor and one of his deacons to visit. On the appointed day, after formal introductions, the deacon held Mr Johnstone's hands and asked, "Do you believe that God can heal you?" Mr Johnstone replied, "Yes."

After his reply, the hymn 'The Great Physician Now is Here' was requested and sung. The pastor and the deacon then laid hands on Mr Johnstone, and after they prayed the pastor anointed him with oil and left.

Shortly after his anointing, Mr Johnstone's general condition began to improve; within a short time he was able to walk again, the sores on his head healed, and his mental state and communication returned to normal. His doctor was amazed at his miraculous improvement and gradually discontinued his medication.

As his condition improved, Mr Johnstone started going out again, and every Sabbath (Saturday) he went to church and could not stop praising God for healing him. He requested baptism and was baptised by the pastor who had prayed and anointed him.

Mr Johnstone's condition improved to such an extent that he was able to travel by train unaided. Wherever he went and whoever he met he would tell them of what God had done for him. Prayer and his faith in God made the difference in his life. He can truly testify that, 'the prayer of faith will save the sick, and the Lord will raise him up.'

Esther's Story - A Call for Help.

"Let your light so shine before men, that they may see your good works and glorify your Father in heaven."

(Matthew 5:16)

Over the years, I developed a very strong bond with my financial consultant. We not only spent time discussing financial issues, but also other concerns. Sometimes, we would make light of some of these and would laugh together. However, I never allowed any of those encounters to go by without sharing my faith with him.

It was February 2004 when I received a telephone call from him. It was not a business call, but a personal call for help. Unknown to me, he had been suffering from diabetes which had now affected his vision. For nearly a year he had been finding it increasingly difficult to see. As a result, his entire life was being seriously affected by his visual impairment. He was unable to drive, experienced problems at work, and was now slipping deep into depression.

As he poured out his heart to me, I listened without interrupting him. As I listened, I felt very sorry for him and encouraged him as best as I could. Before he ended the call, I asked him if I would mind if I prayed with him. He did not hesitate and admitted that anything at that moment would be acceptable. I prayed with him and wished him God's blessing.

Two days after we prayed together, I received another call from a very excited consultant telling me that his vision had dramatically improved. He said that the doctors had told him that his sight would probably return, however, they could not offer him a guarantee or time limit.

Shortly after our telephone conversation I received a letter from him addressed to my church. It was a letter of thanksgiving, thanking God for working through me to bring him hope. In his letter he encouraged the members of the church to continue to reach out to others.

I thank God for what He did. I am daily reminded of the words from the book of Matthew 5:16, "Let your light so shine before men, that they may see your good works and glorify your Father in heaven".

God Provides

Flo's Story - I Believe in Miracles

'And my God shall supply all your needs according to the His riches in glory by Christ Jesus.'

(Philippians 4:19)

I grew up believing in magic, however, when I became an adult and dedicated my life to Christ, I realised that God does not work magic, He is a miracle worker! I was to prove this, over, and over again, as He continues to work miracles in my life.

I can recall one such time when shortly after my mother died, both my husband and I lost our jobs. It was a very difficult time for us. Our situation became more and more distressing. We kept applying for jobs and attending interviews but without success. By this time, we were just about getting by with the bare necessities.

I will never forget that Sunday on our way to church, our eldest daughter asked, "Mommy, what are we having for lunch today?"

"I don't know," I replied, "but God will provide something for us." I felt like Abraham when Isaac asked, "where is the lamb for the burnt offering?" Abraham answered, "God will provide the lamb for the burnt offering, my son."

As we continued our journey to church, I prayed a simple prayer in my heart, "Lord thank you in advance for providing for us. Amen."

We had such a wonderful time at church that, quite honestly, I had forgotten the morning's question from my daughter. However, as we drove home, I began thinking about what we would have to eat for lunch, knowing full well that there wasn't much, if anything, to prepare. On our return home, as we approached the drive, I noticed a large bag on the porch. On alighting from the car, my husband quickly opened it, and to our surprise it was full of groceries! I could hardly contain myself when our daughter shrieked with delight, "Mommy, God has sent us food, He sent us food Mommy!" She was only four years old at the time; it was amazing that she had remembered our earlier conversation.

Words cannot express our gratitude to God, not only did He provide groceries for us, but we had two weeks' supply! To this very day we do not know who left that bag on our porch, but we do know our God whom we serve certainly provided for us that day and still does.

This experience has enlarged our faith and trust in Him. I have shared my story because I want everyone to know that God will always provide no matter what your situation is; call on Him because He is a miracle-working God who will always answer prayers.

Hannah-Mae's Story - Elderberries

'I have been young, and now am old; yet I have not seen the righteous forsaken, nor his descendants begging bread.'

(Psalm 37:25)

We had recently moved to a different part of the country after having bought our first house. I had not yet found a job, but my husband had, however, he was working a long way from home and came home only at weekends. We were struggling financially, but God always provided for our needs. We always had enough to eat.

It was a very hot summer's day and I noticed that there was no drink in the fridge. All we had was water. I knew that my son would be thirsty when he came home from school and would be asking for orange juice to drink, but I didn't even have money to buy a carton of juice! At that moment, words from one of my favourite scriptures came into my mind, 'He will dwell on high; his place of defence will be the fortress of rocks; bread will be given him, his water will be sure.' (Isaiah 33:16) Straightaway, I prayed this prayer, "Dear Lord, please provide something for my son to drink. Amen."

Suddenly, I thought, "I'll go for a walk in the woods to see if I can find some elderberries to make a drink." However, there was not one elderberry in sight. Disappointed, and feeling dejected, I slowly made my way back home. "Why worry," I thought, "when I can pray." This time my prayer was one of thanksgiving, thanking God for providing for me. My disappointment turned to happiness as I contemplated what God would do for me.

I collected my son from school, and as we approached our home, I noticed a carrier bag on the doorstep. I reached forward and picked it up and, to my utter amazement, it contained elderberries! A note was attached to the bag, which said, "I went into the woods today and picked these elderberries and thought you might like to have them." As I held the bag in my hands, I looked up to heaven and said, "Thank you Lord for providing for us." I looked at my son and smiled and said, "Come on, let's go inside and make some elderberry drinks."

As I prepared the elderberries, I could not help thanking and praising God, "You are indeed, 'Jehovah Jireh, the Lord provides."

Jane's Story - The Hidden Bank Account

'And we know that all things work together for good to those who love God, to those who are called according to His purpose.'

(Romans 8:28)

As a divorcee, it was hard bringing up my children and providing for their needs. However, with God's help I managed.

Years after they left home, I received a letter from the Building Society stating that I owed £8,000 on my house. This came as a complete shock because I thought I had paid off the mortgage. I was now a pensioner, and I knew that I would be unable to pay such a large sum of money. However, I sought the Lord in prayer for help and guidance. After considering various options, I decided that I would approach my bank for a loan.

The night before my appointment with the bank manager, the Holy Spirit directed me to my bedside drawer where I kept important papers and documents. As I cleared out unwanted papers, an old bank book that had lain hidden among the papers fell out. I was amazed and could not even recall having had that account. It was such a long time ago that I had completely forgotten about it. I opened the book, and to my utter amazement

I noticed that the balance was £8,000! I was beside myself with joy.

The following day I made my way to the bank and explained to the cashier that I had forgotten that I had the account. She was astonished that I could have forgotten something so important. However, I had an even bigger shock when she told me that the interest alone was able to pay for the amount owed on my house.

This was indeed a miracle! More importantly, God was right on time! He saw my need and at the very moment I needed the money He provided it.

I often wonder how God hid that book from me and how I only found it when I was in great need. Neither can I understand why the bank had not sent me any statements at all. If they had been sending statements I would not have forgotten about the account.

I can only conclude that, "all things work together for good for those who love the Lord." He is truly an awesome God!

Ann's Story - Miracles and More Miracles

'In my distress I cried to the Lord, and He heard me.'

(Psalm 120:1)

My grandmother was the pillar of our family, so it was extremely painful to watch her deteriorate because of the terrible debilitating effects of Alzheimer's disease. Her ability to feed herself, walk, and make coherent sentences, was almost completely gone. However, it was even more devastating when her children decided to put her in a care facility when she was at her most vulnerable.

I desperately wanted to take my grandmother home to live with me so I could care for her. Unfortunately, my financial situation made it impossible. I was also experiencing other significant challenges in my life, which would have made it even more difficult if I were to take her home to live with me.

Each time I visited my grandmother I became more and more concerned for her wellbeing; there were too many questions about her quality of care. She was slowly giving up too. The recurring thought that this is not the way God's children should live in their later years haunted me. However, with my own issues to deal with I was already physically, mentally, and emotionally drained, and clearly there was no way I could give her the best possible care.

It seemed that this situation compelled me to trust God more, and after a few more disturbing incidents that occurred at the care facility, I made the decision that I could not leave my grandmother there any longer. I had to take her home to live with me.

After much prayer and deliberation, I took her home to live with me in my inadequate accommodation, trusting God to take care of everything.

Within months of taking her home to live with me, God provided a spacious four-bedroom house for us, and the money for the deposit, and one month's rent. The house was ideally located, across the road was the local hospital, just walking distance from the pharmacy, a doctor's surgery, and the town centre. He even provided us with the very best doctor in the area. Even though there were many people trying to get on to her list, she immediately accepted my grandmother. This was a much - needed blessing, as she gave my grandmother exceptional treatment. She also discontinued the thirteen different medications that my grandmother had been prescribed in the care home.

God also provided funds for me to hire a practising Christian as a live-in carer for my grandmother. It was one miracle after another. God was answering my prayers in ways that I had not expected! Things just got better; at work He provided me with a new Christian supervisor, who was sympathetic and very supportive. He also provided the local Member of Parliament who was instrumental in helping me to obtain all the benefits that my grandmother was entitled to - appropriate equipment, and the necessary adaptations needed in the house. God also provided my sister, who was already charged with caring for her young family, to help in making the process easier for us.

Although God was working in such miraculous ways, I was still concerned about how I was going to pay my bills; my salary paid for everything, however, it was not enough. My financial situation had not improved, I had a huge credit card bill, I could not even pay the monthly minimum! I was now in arrears. Every penny was spent on my grandmother's care, I had no choice but to stop paying the monthly minimum. I just could not afford it. Throughout these challenges, I never stopped praying.

One day, after I had received another letter threatening to take me to court for non -payment of the council tax, in desperation I cried out to God in prayer. I later called the Benefits Office, seeking a way out, however, they were unable to do anything for at least another three weeks – far too late for the date set for my payment of the council tax. Feeling tired and worn out, I was impressed to go downstairs to open the mail that had landed on my doorstep that morning. I picked up a letter and to my amazement there was a cheque from the Benefits Office for the required amount! (The cheque that I was supposed to wait three weeks for). I could not believe my eyes. It was at that moment that I realised that God had heard and answered my prayer, yet another miracle!

God did not stop there as He continued to work miracles in my life in response to prayer.

For an entire year I had been unable to pay anything on my credit card. I knew that the interest had piled up and very soon I would have to face up to a huge bill. I decided to call the credit card company, and after confirming the card number and my identity, the representative went completely quiet. Her silence worried me, I feared that the bill was so high that she would take some form of immediate action against me. After clearing her throat and pausing for a moment, she informed me that the amount had not increased from the time I ceased making payments. The account was frozen, and the company could not explain why that had happened. They also decided that they were not even going to calculate the amount of interest owed, but I could commence paying from where I left off! I could not believe what I heard. It was God again, answering my prayers in ways I never anticipated.

As I reflect on my experience, I look back in gratitude every day. There are some things that I still can't understand. However, I know that God is a miracle-working God, who took care of my grandmother, and He took care of me in such a way that it has given me confidence to be bold and exercise faith in Him, even when I couldn't see 'the wood for the trees.'

My grandmother has since gone home to rest and is awaiting the return of Jesus Whenever I think of her, I am still overwhelmed by what God did for us, for before I called the answer was on the way.

Helen's Story - God's Plan

'For I know the thoughts that I think toward you, says the Lord, thoughts of peace and not of evil, to give you a future and a hope.'

(Jeremiah 29:11)

It all began in 1986, I was living in a council flat with my three children. I often dreamt of owning my own home. However, there was no way in which I could ever afford to purchase a house. I had no savings, and my job did not pay enough to secure a mortgage.

The longer I lived in the flat, the more I desired to have a place of my own. However, because I had no money, I decided I would apply to the council for a transfer to a house.

My name was placed on the council's transfer list, and I felt confident that it wouldn't be long before I would be transferred. My hopes grew when I noticed that several tenants were being transferred. I thought, surely it wouldn't be long before I would also be moving.

I wanted to be offered a house, but years went by, and no letters came from the council.

Things were about to change when one night I dreamt that I was elderly and still living in the flat. The next morning, I awoke wondering what the dream meant. I believed it was a message from God telling me I would be waiting in vain for a transfer, and if I did not do something to help myself, I would grow old in the flat. It was at that point that I decided to take action.

After taking my children to school that morning, I went straightaway to my local college and enrolled on a one-year part-time foundation course. Although I had received a good education from my country, I felt that since I had not attended school in the United Kingdom, by starting with the foundation course it would enable me to familiarise myself with the British education system.

It was a real struggle trying to study with three children in a small council flat.

After I had completed the foundation course at my local college, I was accepted at a college of Further Education to study for the Access to Social Work course. On completion of this course, I then went on to study at the University of Middlesex. This resulted in six years of very hard study and sacrifices; however, it paid off. I finally graduated, with a degree and a professional qualification in Social Work, in 1992.

By 1993, the council had commenced a new housing scheme where council tenants were given the opportunity to purchase their own house, providing them with a grant for the deposit. I took advantage of the offer and was successful in obtaining a grant that would assist me in getting a mortgage.

In 1995, I heard the 'still small voice', which I had heard before saying, "It's time to buy the house," so I began the search in earnest. I can recall saying to the Lord, "Please show me the house you have provided for me."

After viewing about four houses, which were not suitable, the estate agent told me about a house that had been on the market for six years, and that I should take a look at it. However, when he told me the price, I knew I couldn't afford it and thought it would be a waste of time even viewing it.

However, my friend, who was with me, and the estate agent persuaded me to, at least, take a look at the house. As soon as I opened the gate, I heard the still small voice saying, "This is the house." I immediately turned to my friend who was with me, and said, "This is the house," to which she replied, "I thought you said, you cannot afford this house."

"Yes," I said, "I don't know how, but this is the house." I later made an offer which was accepted.

God provided for me in a miraculous way, and I was able to purchase it. The vendors told me the house had been up for sale twice, the last time being nine years before. I firmly believe that the Lord had set aside that house for me and prevented the sale when I acted on the dream.

The story does not end there. Little did I know that God had something even better in store for me. Unknown to me, His plan was to save me. I grew up in the Caribbean and had attended church during my childhood, but I had not yet committed my life to Him.

After having bought the house, it was another nine years before I gave my life to Christ. It was in 2002, I can remember it was a

Saturday morning, whilst lying on my bed, when I heard that still voice again, saying, "Get up and go to that church." Straight away an image of the church flashed into my mind, and I knew exactly which one it was. It was the Seventh Day Adventist church on Selhurst road in South East London. For several years I had been thinking of attending church, but I wasn't sure which one. I obeyed and attended the church that very same morning.

I was warmly received and from then on became a regular visitor to the church.

I had been attending for several years, when one Sabbath, as I sat in church, I heard the still small voice again saying, "It's time to be baptised." As soon as the service ended, I spoke to an elder and shortly after I began Bible studies and was finally baptised in 2005 and have been an active member ever since. I give God thanks for what He has done in my life.

Reflecting on my journey, I can truly say that God had a plan for my life, but I had to take action for it to be fulfilled. If I had not acted upon the vision He gave me, I would never have known what His plan was for me.

I believe God has a plan for every person's life, however, we need to obey His leading and do our part. When we do, He can do amazing things in our lives. May all praise be given to God our Father whose plan it is to give us hope and a future.

God Cares

Ron's Story – Ride with an Angel
No logical explanation

'There is no one like the God of Jeshurun, who rides the heavens to help you, and in His excellency on the clouds.'

(Deuteronomy 33:26)

It was a Sunday evening when my father had finished preaching at our local church, and we were now on our way home. My brothers and I had walked this way to the church and back many times before with father. It was a long and tiring walk, especially for a nine-year-old boy, as I was then. Once we left the church, the walk was uphill all the way home. Our house stood on a hill.

After having walked for several miles, I soon became very tired. As we approached the steepest hill of the journey, I feared that I would not have enough energy to continue much further. Tiredness had by now gotten the better of me and with a loud sigh, I said, "Dad, I wish that a car would come along right now and give us a lift home." No sooner had I uttered the words than a car, which appeared from nowhere, pulled up alongside us. The driver beckoned for us to get in and we were soon on our way up the hill.

We drove for a while in silence. I noticed the driver kept his eyes firmly on the road; he never spoke. After what appeared to me to have been a long period of silence, father spoke.

"What is your name sir?"

Without as much as glancing at my father, the driver replied, "Why asketh thou my name?" Thereafter we continued our journey in silence.

As for me I was very tired and welcomed the silence. I can recall how peaceful and pleasant the journey was, I felt so safe and secure and just wanted to continue driving for as long as it took. The seats were so comfortable, and before I knew it, I drifted off to sleep.

I was suddenly awakened by the sound of father's voice. He was telling the driver that if he was going to turn left at the approaching junction, we would be happy to walk the rest of the way home. The driver did not reply but continued driving in the direction of our home.

However, on reaching the local Seventh-day Adventist church, he stopped and asked if he could leave us there. Father assured him that it would be quite alright, as the church was not very far from where we lived. We were by now well rested and did not mind walking the short distance to our home. We thanked him and expressed our gratitude as we alighted from the car.

As we turned around to wave a final goodbye, there was no car; it had literally vanished into thin air! My brothers and I stood there with our mouths opened wide, the colour had by now drained from our cheeks, our faces were as white as a sheet. I can remember one of my brothers asking, "Dad, where did the car go? Was this all a dream?"

Father remained silent for a moment, he too seemed to have been in a state of shock. When he finally spoke, he said, (in sombre tones), "Boys, that was angel."

This experience will remain with me and my brother for the rest of our lives. I firmly believe that God sent His angel that evening to take us home. He indeed rides the heavens to help His servants.

Elizabeth's Story - The Carpet Cleaner

'Then I called upon the name of the Lord.'

(Psalm 116:4)

It was a busy Friday morning. As part of the preparations for the Sabbath I had arranged for my carpets to be cleaned. Some young people from my church would be coming for dinner.

I needed extra food, so I quickly drove to the supermarket. However, the trip took longer than anticipated and I found myself with just five minutes to get back home before the carpet cleaner arrived. It was a fifteen-minute journey; there was no way I could make it back on time. Therefore, I did what comes naturally, I presented the problem to God, and prayed a simple prayer, "Lord, you know that even if I broke the speed limit, which I wouldn't do, I will not be able to get home on time, so please delay the carpet cleaner. Thank you."

The journey home was not without challenges, for I encountered heavy traffic which delayed me even more. Finally, I arrived home and there was no carpet cleaner in sight. It seemed as if all my fears were realized. My initial thought was that he had left because there was no one at home. Despondently, I began unpacking the shopping from the car when a van pulled up beside my car. It was the carpet cleaner who apologised for being late. Relieved, I simply smiled at him and told him it was quite alright, because I knew God had heard, and answered, my prayer.

Elizabeth's Story - Trip to South Wales

'It shall come to pass that before they call, I will answer; and while they are still speaking, I will hear.'

(Isaiah 65:24)

I was worried about missing the coach to South Wales. This was going to be my very first time attending a camp meeting, and I was looking forward to attending.

I would have to leave home very early to avoid the morning traffic, and to leave my luggage at the pick-up point, drive back for about ten miles, leave my car on my friend's drive, and then return by public transport to board the coach. Although I left home early and would get to the pick-up point before the appointed time, I began to worry that I would not have enough time to leave my car at the designated spot and then return to catch the coach.

As time went by, the situation was looking more and more impossible as the traffic began to build up. It was at that moment that I decided to pray and ask God to take control of the situation.

I eventually arrived at the pick-up point and bumped into Ellen, my friend who I hadn't seen for many years. She greeted me warmly and in the same breath said, "Let me have your car keys and I'll drop your car off, so you won't miss the coach. I will leave my car in this car park, leave yours where you have planned to leave it, and I'll return by public transport to collect my car." I looked at her in sheer wonder and amazement, it was as if she had read my mind. How did she know? I had not said a word to her about my plan! Still in an almost state of shock, I handed over my keys.

God had gone ahead of me and made all the necessary arrangements. Truly, "before they call, I will answer; while they are still speaking, I will hear." This text has taken on a new meaning for me when I recall the events of that morning.

Ricky's Story - A Very Present Help

'God is our refuge and strength, a very present help in trouble. Therefore, we will not fear, even though the earth be removed, and though the mountains be carried into the midst of the sea; though its waters roar and be troubled, though the mountains shake with its swelling.'

(Psalm 46:1-3)

It was 12:30 pm in Thornton Heath, Surrey. I had gone shopping, and as I made my way back from the shops, I noticed as I approached my car that it had been clamped. On reaching the car, I saw two men walking away. I hastened my footsteps and caught up with them and asked them politely to unclamp my car. They said they would, but I would have to pay them £600.

Knowing that I could not afford £600, I called a friend to see whether he could lend me the money; unfortunately, he was in no position to help. I told the men I had no money and without hesitation they left.

As I sat in my car wondering what I should do, I continued praying, in fact from the moment I realised my car had been clamped, I had begun praying silently for God's intervention. After all, did God not say, that He is a very present help in trouble? So, as I sat in my car wondering what to do, I prayed this simple prayer, "Lord, please help me. Amen."

After praying, I felt quietly confident that God would come to my rescue. So, I sat in the car for about an hour praying and listening to some gospel music. As I sat there, many thoughts ran through my mind. I thought my only option was to let the men take the car away because I had no money to pay them. At that point I began to clear the car of my possessions. However, no sooner had I cleared the car and was about to leave, than to my utter amazement, the two men suddenly appeared from nowhere, and without saying a word to me, began unclamping my car. One of the men appeared angry, however, he assisted his colleague in unclamping the car. Soon the wheel was unclamped, and they calmly walked away and left.

I can still recall sitting in my car in a state of shock. However, once I had gotten over the initial shock, it then dawned on me that God had answered my prayer in front of my very eyes! There and then I bowed my head in gratitude and prayed to the One true God who says, "Call upon Me in the day of trouble; I will deliver you, and you shall glorify Me." (Psalm 50:15)

To this day, I will never understand why the men returned, but this I do know, whenever I recall the incident, I cannot help myself from praising God and giving thanks. Often, I marvel at God's faithfulness and a smile breaks over my face as I give thanks to Him.

I certainly learned that day, how important it is to trust in Jesus.

Ruth's Story - When You Least Expect A Mother's Prayer

'Likewise, the Spirit also helps in our weaknesses. For we do not know what we should pray for as we ought, but the Spirit Himself makes intercession for us with groanings which cannot be uttered.'

(Romans 8:26)

It was June 2007, when the answer came.

When I discovered that my son was smoking it distressed me greatly. I tried everything to get him to stop, but to no avail. Frustrated, angry, and feeling powerless, I finally heeded my sister's advice to, "Stop talking and start praying." I turned to God and began praying earnestly for Him to break my son's smoking habit.

One day, after having prayed for many years, the Holy Spirit revealed to me that I was praying incorrectly, and instructed me how I should pray. I was reminded by St. Paul in Romans 8:26 that it is the Spirit Himself who makes intercession for us with "groanings which cannot be uttered."

After this revelation, I prayed this prayer, "Dear Lord, thank you for revealing to me how I should pray. Please make my son's smoking habit so abhorrent to him that even the smell of tobacco will make him sick. AMEN."

I prayed this prayer throughout the month of June 2007. My son at this time was working abroad, and unknown to me then, was smoking forty cigarettes daily! That's two hundred and eighty per week!

It was now July, and on his birthday, he called me. He didn't even give me the chance to wish him happy birthday when he excitedly announced, "Mom, do you know what? I have given up smoking, and even the very smell of it makes me sick!"

I could not contain myself, and kept on shouting, "Thank You God. Thank You." The very words that I had prayed to the Lord when instructed by the Holy Spirit, were the very words he was repeating to me.

This experience has taught me to always take everything to God in prayer and to be persistent even though it would appear He's taking a long time to answer.

www.ingramcontent.com/pod-product-compliance
Lightning Source LLC
Chambersburg PA
CBHW011803040426
42450CB00018B/3454